Christmas GOODIES

Edible gifts for the festive season

THE AUSTRALIAN Women's Weekly

contents

Christmas is an occasion to indulge as we celebrate with family and friends, and what better way to celebrate than by giving handmade gifts. Whip up some shortbread, nougat and fruit mince or get crafty with decorations. Whatever you make will be enjoyed by your loved ones into the new year.

Editorial & Food Director

Pamela Clark

sweet treats

You will definitely want to keep the cookie jar full of these delicious biscuits and slices. Make a double batch so you also have enough to give as gifts.

Tips Rocky road can be made a week ahead, keep refrigerated in an airtight container. To make this treat for children, swap turkish delight for raspberry jubes and the nuts for chocolate-coated Clinkers.

gourmet rocky road

- 450g (14½ ounces) white chocolate
- 300g (9½ ounces) white marshmallows, chopped coarsely
- ¼ cup (20g) shredded coconut, toasted
- 400g (12½ ounces) turkish delight, chopped coarsely
- ¼ cup (40g) unsalted roasted almonds, chopped coarsely
- ½ cup (75g) roasted pistachios

1 Grease two 8cm x 26cm (3¼-inch x 10½-inch) bar cake pans; line base and sides with baking paper, extending paper 5cm (2 inches) above long sides.
2 Stir chocolate in a medium heatproof bowl over a medium saucepan of simmering water until smooth (don't let water touch base of bowl).

3 Combine marshmallow, coconut, turkish delight and nuts in a large bowl. Working quickly, stir in chocolate; spread mixture into pans, push down to flatten. Refrigerate until set then cut as desired.

makes 36
prep + cook time
20 minutes (+ refrigeration)

spiced wreath biscuits

- 125g (4 ounces) butter, softened
- ½ cup (110g) firmly packed brown sugar
- ½ cup (125ml) treacle
- 1 egg, separated
- 2 cups (300g) plain (all-purpose) flour
- ½ cup (75g) self-raising flour
- 1 teaspoon bicarbonate of soda (baking soda)
- 2 teaspoons ground ginger
- 1 teaspoon ground cinnamon
- ¼ teaspoon ground cardamom
- 2 tablespoons raw sugar
- ⅓ cup (25g) flaked almonds

1 Preheat oven to 180°C/350°F. Line oven trays with baking paper.
2 Beat butter, brown sugar, treacle and egg yolk in a small bowl with an electric mixer until pale and creamy. Transfer to a large bowl. Stir in sifted flours, soda and spices. Turn dough onto a floured surface, knead until smooth. Cover with plastic wrap, refrigerate 30 minutes.

3 Divide dough into two portions; roll each portion separately on a lightly floured surface until 4mm (⅛-inch) thick. Cut out rounds using a 7cm (3-inch) fluted cutter. Use a 3cm (1¼-inch) fluted cutter to cut an inner circle from each disc. Transfer to trays.
4 Brush tops of dough with lightly beaten egg white; sprinkle half the biscuits with raw sugar and remaining biscuits with nuts. Bake about 10 minutes or until browned lightly. Stand 5 minutes, then transfer to wire racks to cool.

> **makes** 40
> **prep + cook time**
> 1 hour (+ refrigeration)

Tip Biscotti will keep in an airtight container for at least a month.

lemon, honey & pistachio biscotti

- ½ cup (110g) caster (superfine) sugar
- 1 egg
- ¾ cup (110g) plain (all-purpose) flour
- ⅓ cup (50g) self-raising flour
- 2 teaspoons finely grated lemon rind
- ½ cup (70g) unsalted pistachios, roasted
- ¼ cup (50g) pepitas (pumpkin seed kernels)
- ¼ cup (35g) sunflower seed kernels
- 1 tablespoon honey
- 2 teaspoons caster (superfine) sugar, extra

1 Preheat oven to 180°C/350°F. Grease an oven tray.

2 Whisk sugar and egg in a medium bowl until combined; stir in sifted flours and rind, then nuts, seeds and honey. Shape dough on a lightly floured work surface into a 20cm (8-inch) log; place on tray. Sprinkle with extra sugar; bake for 30 minutes or until golden. Cool on tray.

3 Reduce oven temperature to 150°C/300°F.

4 Using a serrated knife, cut log diagonally into 5mm (¼-inch) slices. Place slices, in a single layer, on ungreased oven trays. Bake biscotti for 20 minutes or until dry and crisp, turning halfway through baking time. Cool on wire racks.

makes 40
prep + cook time
1 hour 15 minutes
(+ cooling)

tips Recipe can be made a month ahead; store in an airtight container. Australian wattleseeds have a coffee-like aroma and a toasted flavour. They are available from select supermarkets and delis. If you can't find wattleseeds, substitute with ground coffee.

wattleseed & orange shortbread

- 250g (8 ounces) butter, softened
- ⅓ cup (75g) caster (superfine) sugar
- 2 teaspoons ground toasted wattleseeds
- 2 teaspoons finely grated orange rind
- 2 cups (300g) plain (all-purpose) flour
- ½ cup (100g) rice flour
- 2 tablespoons caster (superfine) sugar, extra

makes 24
prep + cook time
1 hour (+ refrigeration)

1 Preheat oven to 150°C/300°F. Grease two large oven trays; line with baking paper.
2 Beat butter, sugar, wattleseeds and rind in a small bowl with an electric mixer until combined. Add large spoonfuls of combined sifted flours to butter mixture, beating after each addition.
3 Press ingredients together; knead gently on a floured surface until smooth. Divide dough into half; cover with plastic, refrigerate 1 hour.
4 Roll one dough half on a piece of floured baking paper until 14cm x 30cm (5½ inches x 12 inches) and 4mm (¼-inch) thick. Using a small sharp knife (or leaf-shaped biscuit cutter), cut out gumleaf shapes; place on trays. Using the back of a knife, mark a line for the centre vein. Repeat with remaining dough.
5 Bake for 18 minutes or until dry and pale in colour. Sprinkle hot shortbread with extra sugar; cool on trays.

Tips Loosely cover the blondies with foil if the almonds are browning too quickly. Store in an airtight container for up to 1 week.

Christmas blondies

- 2 tablespoons brandy
- ⅔ cup (220g) bottled fruit mince
- 180g (5½ ounces) butter, softened
- 1 teaspoon vanilla extract
- 1 cup (220g) firmly packed brown sugar
- 2 eggs
- 1 cup (150g) plain (all-purpose) flour
- ½ cup (75g) self-raising flour
- ½ cup (60g) ground almonds
- ½ cup (95g) white Choc Bits
- 1¼ cups (100g) flaked almonds, lightly toasted

makes 16
prep + cook time 1 hour

1 Preheat oven to 180°C/350°F. Grease a deep 20cm (8-inch) square cake pan; line base and sides with baking paper.

2 Combine brandy and fruit mince in a small bowl.

3 Beat butter, extract and sugar in a small bowl with an electric mixer until pale. Add eggs; beat until combined, then add sifted flours and almonds; beat on low speed until combined.

4 Stir in fruit mince mixture, chocolate and half the nuts. Spread mixture into pan; sprinkle with remaining nuts.

5 Bake 40 minutes or until a skewer inserted into the centre comes out with a few crumbs attached. Cool in pan. Turn out, then cut into squares.

6 Serve dusted with sifted icing sugar, if you like.

gift wrapping

Gift-giving is hugely rewarding for both the giver and the receiver. Taking the time to personally wrap a gift shows that you've put thought and care into what you're giving. And let's not forget the joy of untying the ribbons and carefully unfolding the paper or rustling tissue that encloses a gift. Gift wrapping can be the celebration of a special occasion.

The key to wrapping the perfect gift is to start by cutting the paper to the correct size; too much paper creates a badly wrapped present. The simplest way to work out how much paper you need is to lay the gift on the wrapping paper and roll it across three times, adding an overlap. Use scissors to cut paper to this length then wrap your gift firmly – sharply creased edges and corners produce a polished finish.

By far the easiest way to wrap a gift is to enclose it in a box then decorate the box. Source a variety of different sized boxes then choose a colour theme for your decorations; for Christmas, we chose red, white and stone. Look for contrasting fabrics, coloured paper, ribbons and buttons in these colours to add a little flare.

Using the photographs as a guide, position fabric, paper, ribbons and buttons on boxes. Glue or tape decorations to boxes to achieve desired effect.

Pinking shears give a decorative edge to fabric and paper. You can buy them from haberdashery and craft stores, although they can be expensive.

Tip A cheaper option is scissors with various edgings used for paper crafts. When cut on paper, they create myriad different patterns.

white Christmas

- **500g (1 pound) white chocolate, chopped coarsely**
- **1 cup (35g) rice bubbles**
- **1 cup (160g) sultanas**
- **1 cup (140g) macadamias, roasted, chopped coarsely**
- **1 cup (160g) finely chopped dried apricots**
- **1 cup (130g) dried sweetened cranberries**
- **¾ cup (105g) pistachios, roasted, chopped coarsely**
- **1 teaspoon ground cardamom**

1 Grease a 20cm x 30cm (8 inch x 12 inch) rectangular slice pan; line base and long sides with baking paper, extending paper 5cm (2 inches) over sides.

2 Melt chocolate in a large heatproof bowl over a large saucepan of simmering water (do not let water touch base of bowl). Remove from heat; quickly stir in remaining ingredients.

3 Press mixture firmly into pan. Refrigerate for 2 hours or until firm. Cut into pieces to serve.

makes 32
prep + cook time
20 minutes
(+ refrigeration)

Tips Swap the dried fruit for glacé fruit — try glacé pineapple and ginger. Store white Christmas in an airtight container in the refrigerator for up to 1 month.

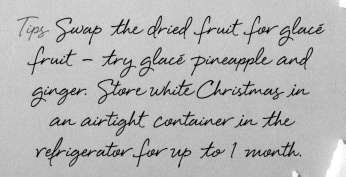

angel gift tag cookies

- **125g (4 ounces) butter, softened**
- **¾ cup (165g) caster (superfine) sugar**
- **1 egg**
- **1¾ cups (260g) plain (all-purpose) flour**
- **⅓ cup (50g) self-raising flour**
- **2 tablespoons white (granulated) sugar**
- **red ribbon**

lemon royal icing
- **2 cups (320g) pure icing (confectioners') sugar**
- **1 egg white**
- **2 teaspoons lemon juice**

makes 20
prep + cook time
50 minutes
(+ refrigeration & standing)

1 Beat butter, caster sugar and egg in a small bowl with an electric mixer until light and fluffy. Stir in sifted flours in two batches. Knead dough on a floured surface until smooth. Cover with plastic wrap; refrigerate 30 minutes.

2 Preheat oven to 180°C/350°F. Line two oven trays with baking paper.

3 Roll dough between sheets of baking paper to 5mm (¼-inch) thickness. Cut 20 x 8cm x 11cm (3¼-inch x 4½-inch) angels from dough; cut two 2cm (¾-inch) moon shapes across centre of angels for threading ribbon. Place on oven trays.

4 Bake cookies about 12 minutes. Cool on trays.

5 Meanwhile, make lemon royal icing.

6 Spread angel cookies with icing; sprinkle with white sugar. Stand at room temperature until icing is set; thread ribbon through holes.

lemon royal icing Sift icing sugar through a fine sieve onto a sheet of baking paper. Beat egg white in a small bowl with electric mixer until foamy; beat in icing sugar 1 tablespoon at a time. Stir in juice.

Tips Angel cookie cutters are available online or from cake decorating stores. Store cookies in an airtight container for up to 2 days.

tips A sugar (candy) thermometer, available from kitchenware stores, is essential for this recipe. Nougat can be made a week ahead. Store in an airtight container between layers of baking paper in a cool, dry place. If the weather is humid, make close to serving.

cranberry, almond & cherry nougat

- 2 sheets edible rice paper
- vegetable oil or cooking-oil spray
- 1 cup (220g) caster (superfine) sugar
- 2 tablespoons glucose syrup
- 2 tablespoons honey
- 2 tablespoons water
- 1 egg white
- ½ cup (80g) roasted almond kernels, chopped coarsely
- ½ cup (65g) dried sweetened cranberries
- ⅓ cup (70g) green glacé cherries, quartered

makes 6
prep + cook time
1 hour (+ cooling)

1 Cut rice paper into 12 rounds to fit six 7.5cm (3-inch) egg rings. Grease inside of egg rings. Place egg rings on a baking paper-lined oven tray. Place one rice paper round in each egg ring.
2 Combine sugar, glucose, honey and the water in a small heavy-based saucepan; stir over low heat, without boiling, until sugar is completely dissolved. Brush down the side of the pan with a pastry brush dipped in hot water to dissolve all the sugar crystals.
3 Boil, uncovered, without stirring, until syrup reaches 154°C on a sugar thermometer, remove immediately from heat.

4 Just before syrup is ready, beat egg white in a small heatproof bowl with an electric mixer until soft peaks form. With mixer operating, add hot syrup to egg white in a thin steady stream. Beat until all syrup is added (mixture will be firm and sticky).
5 Working quickly, stir nuts, cranberries and cherries into egg white mixture. Using an oiled metal spatula (or oiled hands if not too hot), quickly press mixture into an egg ring, press a rice paper round on top. Repeat with remaining mixture and rice paper. Stand 5 minutes before removing egg rings. Cool completely before storing in an airtight container. Cut in half to serve, if you like.

Christmas tree shortbread

- 250g (8 ounces) butter
- 1 teaspoon vanilla extract
- ½ cup (80g) icing (confectioners') sugar
- 1¼ cups (185g) plain (all-purpose) flour
- ½ cup (75g) cornflour (cornstarch)
- 125g (4 ounces) dark (semi-sweet) chocolate, chopped coarsely
- 125g (4 ounces) white chocolate, chopped coarsely
- cachous, sugar pearls and confetti sprinkles

makes 15
prep + cook time
45 minutes
(+ refrigeration & cooling)

1 Line two oven trays with baking paper.

2 Beat butter, extract and sugar in a small bowl with an electric mixer until light and fluffy; beat in sifted flour and cornflour until combined. Enclose in plastic wrap; refrigerate 30 minutes.

3 Preheat oven to 180°C/350°F.

4 Roll dough between sheets of baking paper until 5mm (¼-inch) thick, place on tray; refrigerate 15 minutes.

5 Cut 15 x 11cm (4½-inch) christmas trees from dough, re-rolling scraps as necessary; place on trays about 1cm (½ inch) apart. Bake about 15 minutes; cool on trays.

6 Melt both chocolates, separately, in small heatproof bowls over small saucepans of simmering water (don't let water touch base of bowls).

7 Holding tree trunks over pan, spoon chocolate over one side of trees (not trunks), drain off excess. Return to trays; decorate trees with cachous, pearls and sprinkles. Refrigerate until set.

tips Melt one type of chocolate at a time and coat half the number of trees before melting and coating the remaining trees. Decorate the trees before the chocolate sets.

tips Marshmallows can be made 2 days ahead. They will keep, refrigerated, in an airtight container for up to 2 weeks. It is best to cut the marshmallows using an oiled knife.

passionfruit marshmallow

- 4 passionfruit
- 2 tablespoons powdered gelatine
- 1 cup (250ml) water
- 2 cups (440g) caster (superfine) sugar
- 2 tablespoons vodka
- red and yellow food colouring
- 1½ cups (120g) desiccated coconut

makes 24
prep + cook time
1 hour 15 minutes
(+ refrigeration)

1 Remove pulp from passionfruit. Using the pulse button, process pulp in a food processor for 15 seconds to loosen juice from seeds; strain through a fine sieve, pressing down firmly on seeds to extract all juice. Measure juice; you will need ¼ cup (60ml).

2 Place juice in a small cup; sprinkle over gelatine, stir to combine (mixture will be thick).

3 Stir the water and sugar in a medium saucepan over medium heat, without boiling, until sugar dissolves. Bring to the boil; stir in gelatine mixture and vodka. Boil for 20 minutes, remove from heat; cool for 10 minutes.

4 Pour mixture into a medium bowl of an electric mixer; beat on high speed for 15 minutes or until mixture is very thick and white. Tint marshmallow mixture yellow and red with food colouring to make a pale orange colour.

5 Rinse a deep 20cm (8-inch) square cake pan with cold water; do not dry. Pour marshmallow mixture into pan; refrigerate for 3 hours or until set.

6 Remove marshmallow from pan; cut into 24 squares. Toss squares into coconut to coat.

bottled & sealed

Whether it is sweet or savoury, classic Christmas fare only needs a hint of spice. Your homemade marmalade and chutney will be a favourite under the tree.

Tip Muesli will keep refrigerated in an airtight container for up to 2 months.

maple &
pistachio muesli

- ½ cup (125ml) maple syrup
- ⅓ cup (80ml) light olive oil
- 4 cups (360g) rolled oats
- ⅔ cup (80g) oat bran
- ½ cup (50g) walnuts, chopped coarsely
- ½ cup (70g) unsalted pistachios
- 2 tablespoons sesame seeds
- 1 cup (130g) dried sweetened cranberries
- ½ cup (80g) dried currants
- ½ cup (75g) finely chopped dried apricots

1 Preheat oven to 140°C/280°F.
2 Combine syrup and oil in a small bowl.
3 Combine oats, bran, nuts and seeds in a large bowl. Stir in syrup mixture; mix well. Spread evenly onto two shallow oven trays. Roast for 35 minutes, stirring occasionally.

4 Add dried fruits to mixture; stir to combine, roast a further 5 minutes or until browned lightly.
5 Cool muesli completely on trays, before packing into airtight jars or containers.

makes 8 cups
prep + cook time
45 minutes (+ cooling)

dukkah

- ⅔ cup (110g) blanched almonds
- ⅔ cup (110g) hazelnuts
- ½ cup (75g) sesame seeds
- ¼ cup (20g) coriander seeds
- 2 tablespoons cumin seeds
- 2 teaspoons freshly ground black pepper
- 2 teaspoons flaked sea salt

1 Preheat oven to 180°C/350°F.

2 Spread nuts on an oven tray; roast for 10 minutes or until almonds are golden and hazelnut skins have split. Place hazelnuts onto a clean tea towel; rub nuts to remove as much of the skin as possible; cool.

3 Meanwhile, place sesame seeds in a dry medium frying pan over low heat; cook, stirring continuously, until golden. Transfer immediately to a large heatproof bowl; cool.

4 Process nuts until chopped finely; add to sesame seeds in bowl.

5 Combine coriander and cumin seeds in same dry frying pan; cook over low heat, stirring occasionally, until fragrant. Cool, then grind using a mortar and pestle or spice grinder. Add seeds to nut mixture with pepper and salt; mix well. Store in airtight jars.

makes 2½ cups
prep + cook time
40 minutes

flavoured salts

lemon & chilli salt

- 2 medium lemons (280g)
- 1 cup (125g) sea salt flakes
- 2 teaspoons dried
  oregano leaves
- 2 teaspoons dried
  chilli flakes

1 Remove rind from lemons with a zester or peel lemons thinly with a vegetable peeler, avoiding the white pith. Cut rind into thin strips.
2 Combine rind with salt and oregano in a medium frying pan; stir over low heat for 3 minutes or until rind is dry. Remove from the heat; stir in chilli; cool.

tips Salt will keep in an airtight container for up to 2 months. Sprinkle over chicken or fish.

makes 1 cup
prep + cook time
5 minutes (+ cooling)

orange & fennel salt

- 1 medium orange (240g)
- 1 cup (125g) sea salt flakes
- 2 teaspoons fennel seeds
- ½ teaspoon ground
  white pepper

1 Remove rind from orange with a zester or peel orange thinly with a vegetable peeler, avoiding the white pith. Cut rind into thin strips.
2 Combine rind with remaining ingredients in a medium frying pan; stir over low heat for 3 minutes or until rind is dry. Remove from the heat; cool.

tips Salt will keep in an airtight container for up to 2 months. Sprinkle over pork, fish or duck.

makes 1 cup
prep + cook time
5 minutes (+ cooling)

Tip These nuts tend to clump together but will keep in an airtight container for up to a week.

honey soy nuts

- 1¼ cups (150g) pecans
- 1 cup (150g) raw cashews
- 1 cup (160g) natural almonds
- ⅓ cup (65g) pepitas (pumpkin seed kernels)
- ⅓ cup (50g) sunflower seed kernels
- 1 tablespoon sesame seeds
- 1 tablespoon nigella seeds
- 1 teaspoon finely chopped fresh rosemary
- 1 teaspoon cayenne pepper
- 1 teaspoon freshly ground black pepper
- ½ teaspoon sea salt flakes
- ¼ cup (90g) honey
- 2 tablespoons sunflower oil
- 1 tablespoon soy sauce

1 Preheat oven to 180°C/350°F. Line a large oven tray with baking paper.

2 Combine nuts, seeds, rosemary, peppers and salt in a large heatproof bowl.

3 Place honey, oil and soy sauce in a small saucepan; stir over low heat until combined and honey has thinned. Pour honey mixture over nut mixture; stir to combine.

4 Spread nut mixture on tray; roast, in the oven, for 20 minutes, stirring halfway through cooking time, or until cashews are golden in colour; cool.

makes 3½ cups
prep + cook time
30 minutes

table setting

placemats

Randomly sew red buttons in various shapes and sizes along one side of a placemat, as pictured above.

piñatas

Trace large star shapes on brown paper sandwich bags. Leaving one side open, machine stitch (running stitch or tacking is fine) around the edge of the star. Cut around the star, about 5mm (¼-inch) from the stiches. Fill the bags with lollies, then sew up the opening.

Tip Attach a loop to each piñata and hang on the Christmas tree.

place cards

Cut lightweight white cardboard to the required size. Fold each card in half. Glue red buttons in various shapes and sizes in bottom right hand corner of place cards to achieve desired effect.

candles

Cut semi-transparent red, white and stone-coloured paper to heights of clear glasses in various shapes and sizes. Wrap paper around glasses and secure with double-sided sticky tape. Place tea lights in glasses.

Tip If using tall glasses, you will need extra long matches to safely light the candles. These are available from camping stores and supermarkets.

makes 9½ cups
prep + cook time
30 minutes (+ standing)

cranberry & apple fruit mince

- 2⅔ cups (325g) dried cranberries
- 2½ cups (200g) finely chopped dried apples
- 2 cups (320g) finely chopped raisins
- 1 cup (250g) finely chopped dried cherries
- ¾ cup (150g) finely chopped dried figs
- ½ cup (85g) mixed peel
- ½ cup (115g) glacé ginger, chopped finely
- 3 medium apples (450g), peeled, grated coarsely
- 1½ cups (330g) firmly packed brown sugar
- ½ cup (160g) raspberry jam
- 1 tablespoon finely grated orange rind
- ¼ cup (60ml) orange juice
- 2 teaspoons mixed spice
- ½ teaspoon ground clove
- 1 cinnamon stick, halved
- 1⅓ cups (330ml) Grand Marnier

1 Mix ingredients in a large bowl until combined.
2 Cover bowl with plastic wrap. Store mixture in a cool dry place for a month before using; stir mixture every two or three days.
3 Place clean jars and lids in a large saucepan; cover completely with cold water. Bring to the boil, covered, for 20 minutes. Remove jars and lids carefully from the water; drain jars upright (to allow the water to evaporate) on the sink until dry.
4 Spoon mixture into sterilised jars; seal. Store in the refrigerator.

tips Fruit mince makes a beautiful gift. It will keep in the refrigerator for at least 12 months. If you can't find dried cherries, use extra dried cranberries instead.

citrus marmalade

- 4 large oranges (1.2kg)
- 3 medium lemons (420g)
- 4 large limes (400g)
- 1.25 litres (5 cups) water
- 1.6kg (7 cups) white (granulated) sugar, approximately

1 Peel fruit thinly; cut rind into thin strips. Remove pith from fruit; reserve half and discard remaining pith. Chop flesh coarsely; reserve seeds.

2 Combine flesh and rind in a large bowl with the water. Tie reserved pith and seeds in muslin; add to bowl. Stand at room temperature overnight.

3 Place fruit mixture and muslin bag in a large saucepan; bring to the boil. Simmer, covered, for 25 minutes or until rind is soft. Discard muslin bag.

4 Measure fruit mixture; allow 1 cup (220g) sugar for each cup of mixture. Return mixture and sugar to pan; stir over medium heat, without boiling, until sugar dissolves. Boil, uncovered, for 40 minutes or until marmalade sets on a cold saucer.

5 Pour marmalade into hot sterilised jars (see method, page 41); seal immediately.

makes 7 cups
prep + cook time 1 hour 35 minutes (+ standing)

Tips Marmalade will keep for up to 1 year unopened. Add about 1 tablespoon marmalade to a 125g butter mix for a Christmas cake with a delicate citrus undertone.

Tips Store chilli oil in a cool dark place for 3 months. Use in stir-frying or to add flavour to steak or chicken.

chilli oil

- 3 cups (750ml) extra virgin olive oil
- 1/3 cup (25g) chilli flakes

makes 3 cups
prep + cook time
10 minutes (+ standing)

1 Warm oil in a medium saucepan over low heat for 4 minutes or until small bubbles appear on bottom of saucepan. Remove from heat, stir in chilli flakes. Cover, stand at room temperature for at least 24 hours.

2 Strain oil through muslin or paper towel-lined sieve into sterilised bottles (see method, page 41); seal. Discard chilli flakes.

Tips Refrigerate liqueur for up to 6 months. Label and date jars when cold.

irish crème liqueur

- 1 tablespoon instant coffee granules
- 1 tablespoon boiling water
- 1½ tablespoons chocolate-flavoured topping
- 350ml irish whiskey
- 1¾ cups (460ml) pouring cream
- 395g (12½ ounces) canned condensed milk
- 1 egg
- 1 teaspoon coconut essence

1 Dissolve coffee in the water in a large jug; stir in topping.
2 Whisk in remaining ingredients. Strain mixture into cooled sterilised bottles (see method, page 41); seal immediately.

makes 5 cups
prep time 10 minutes

tomato & lemon myrtle chutney

- 2kg (4 pounds) green tomatoes, cored, chopped coarsely
- 2 large brown onions (400g), chopped coarsely
- 2 large green apples (400g), peeled, cored, chopped coarsely
- 2 cups (440g) raw sugar
- 2½ cups (625ml) apple cider vinegar
- 1 cup (150g) sultanas
- 3 fresh long red chillies, chopped finely
- 6 cloves garlic, chopped finely
- 2 teaspoons sea salt flakes
- ½ teaspoon ground lemon myrtle

1 Stir ingredients in a large saucepan over high heat, without boiling, until sugar dissolves; bring to the boil. Reduce heat to medium-low; simmer, uncovered, stirring occasionally, for 2 hours or until chutney is thick.
2 Spoon hot chutney into hot sterilised jars (see method, page 41); seal immediately. Store in a cool, dark place for at least 3 weeks before opening. Refrigerate after opening.

tip Lemon myrtle is a native Australian herb with an intense but pleasant lemony taste without the acidity. Substitute 1 teaspoon finely grated lemon rind or 2 very thinly sliced kaffir lime leaves.

brandied cumquats

- **750g (1½ pounds) cumquats**
- **2 cinnamon sticks, halved lengthways**
- **2 vanilla beans, halved lengthways**
- **3 cups (660g) caster (superfine) sugar**
- **2½ cups (625ml) brandy**

makes 7 cups
prep time 10 minutes (+ standing)

1 Wash and dry cumquats well, prick each one several times with a fine skewer or a thick needle.
2 Place cumquats, cinnamon and vanilla beans into sterilised jars (see method, page 41); pour over enough of the combined sugar and brandy to cover cumquats completely. Seal.

3 Stand the jars in a cool, dark place for at least 2 months before using. Invert the jars every few days to help dissolve the sugar.

tips Buy cumquats when they are in season (autumn to spring). Serve brandied cumquats with ice-cream or use them in pies, puddings, cakes and crumbles. Drink the flavoured brandy as you would a liqueur.

little cakes

What is Christmas without fruit cake and puddings? Enjoy a little bite of the festive season with these individual portions. They're also perfect as gifts.

rich eggless
boiled fruit cakes

- 750g (1½ pounds) mixed dried fruit
- 1 cup (250ml) water
- ½ cup (110g) firmly packed dark brown sugar
- 90g (3 ounces) butter
- 1 cup (150g) plain (all-purpose) flour
- ½ cup (75g) self-raising flour
- ½ teaspoon bicarbonate of soda (baking soda)
- 1 teaspoon mixed spice
- ¼ cup (60ml) sweet sherry, rum or brandy
- 2 tablespoons sweet sherry, rum or brandy, extra

1 Combine fruit, the water, sugar and butter in a large saucepan; stir over medium heat until sugar dissolves. Cover; simmer for 3 minutes. Remove from heat; stand until cold.

2 Preheat oven to 150°C/300°F. Place two paper cases in each hole of a six-hole (¾-cup/180ml) texas muffin pan.

3 Stir sifted dry ingredients alternately with sherry into the cold fruit mixture; mix well. Divide mixture between pan holes. Bake about 1 hour 15 minutes. Brush hot cakes evenly with extra sherry. Turn cakes, top-side up, onto a wire rack to cool.

tip The double cases protect the mixture from drying out during the long baking time.

makes 6
prep + cook time
1 hour 45 minutes
(+ standing & cooling)

iced Christmas cupcakes

- 500g (1 pound) mixed dried fruit
- 125g (4 ounces) butter, chopped coarsely
- ½ cup (125ml) water
- 1 cup (200g) firmly packed dark brown sugar
- ¼ teaspoon bicarbonate of soda (baking soda)
- 2 tablespoons brandy
- 2 eggs, beaten lightly
- ½ cup (75g) plain (all-purpose) flour
- ½ cup (75g) self-raising flour
- ½ cup (75g) cornflour (cornstarch), for dusting
- 750g (1½ pounds) white ready-made icing
- 1 egg white, beaten lightly

makes 12
prep + cook time
2 hours (+ cooling)

1 Combine fruit, butter, the water, sugar and soda in a large saucepan; stir over medium heat until butter melts and sugar dissolves. Bring to the boil; remove from heat, stir in brandy. Transfer to a large heatproof bowl; cool to room temperature.

2 Preheat oven to 150°C/300°F. Line two six-hole (¾-cup/180ml) texas muffin pans with paper cases.

3 Stir eggs into fruit mixture, then the sifted flours; divide mixture evenly among pan holes. Bake for 40 minutes or until a skewer inserted into the centre comes out clean. Cover hot cakes with a clean tea towel while still in the pan; cool cakes in pan.

4 On a surface dusted with cornflour, knead icing until smooth. Roll out into a 5mm (¼-inch) thickness. Using a 5.5cm (2¼-inch) fluted cutter, cut out 12 rounds. Lightly brush tops of cakes with egg white; cover with icing rounds.

5 Using remaining icing, cut out snowflake shapes and the letters to spell 'noel'. Paint letters with edible gold paint. When completely dry, brush the letters with egg white; secure to cakes. Brush snowflakes with egg white, then secure on top of icing of remaining cakes.

tip To decorate, you will need alphabet and snowflake cutters, edible gold paint, available from cake decorator supply shops, and a new small artist's paintbrush.

mini brandy
apricot puddings

You need six 30cm (12-inch) squares of unbleached calico and six 1m (1 yard) lengths of kitchen string.

- 1 cup (170g) raisins, chopped coarsely
- 1 cup (160g) sultanas
- 1 cup (150g) finely chopped seeded dried dates
- ½ cup (95g) finely chopped seeded prunes
- ½ cup (85g) mixed peel
- ½ cup (125g) finely chopped glacé apricots
- 1 teaspoon finely grated lemon rind
- 2 tablespoons lemon juice
- 2 tablespoons apricot jam
- 2 tablespoons brandy
- 250g (8 ounces) butter, softened
- 2 cups (440g) firmly packed brown sugar
- 5 eggs
- 1¼ cups (185g) plain (all-purpose) flour
- ½ teaspoon ground nutmeg
- ½ teaspoon mixed spice
- 4 cups (280g) stale breadcrumbs
- 1 cup (150g) plain (all-purpose) flour, extra

1 Combine fruit, rind, juice, jam and brandy in a large bowl; mix well. Cover tightly with plastic wrap; store in a cool, dark place for one week, stirring every day.

2 Beat butter and sugar in a small bowl with an electric mixer until combined; beat in eggs one at a time. Add butter mixture to fruit mixture, mix well, then mix in sifted dry ingredients and breadcrumbs.

3 Fill a boiler three-quarters full with hot water, cover with a tight lid; bring to the boil. Wearing thick rubber gloves, dip calico squares, one at a time, into boiling water; boil 1 minute then remove, squeeze excess water from cloth. Spread hot cloths on bench, rub 2 tablespoons of extra flour into centre of each cloth to cover an area about 18cm (7¼-inch) in diameter, leaving flour a little thicker in centre where pudding 'skin' needs to be thickest.

4 Divide pudding mixture among cloths; placing in centre of each cloth. Gather cloths around mixture, avoiding any deep pleats; pat into round shapes. Tie cloths tightly with string as close to mixture as possible.

5 Lower puddings into the boiling water; tie ends of string to handles of boiler to suspend puddings. Cover, boil 2 hours, replenishing water as necessary.

6 Place wooden spoons through string loops, suspend from spoon by placing over rungs of upturned stool; hang 10 minutes.

7 Transfer puddings to board; cut string, carefully peel back cloth. Turn puddings onto a plate then carefully peel cloth away completely; cool. Stand at least 20 minutes or until skin darkens and pudding becomes firm.

makes 6
prep + cook time
3 hours (+ standing time)

tips Serve cakes warm or cold with cream or ice-cream. Cakes will keep in an airtight container in the refrigerator for 2 days. Reheat in microwave on MEDIUM (50% power) for 10 second bursts until just warm.

glacé fruit cakes with ginger syrup

- ¾ cup (105g) slivered almonds
- 90g (3 ounces) butter, softened
- 2 teaspoons finely grated lemon rind
- ¾ cup (165g) caster (superfine) sugar
- 2 eggs
- ¾ cup (110g) plain (all-purpose) flour
- ½ cup (75g) self-raising flour
- ⅓ cup (80ml) milk
- 4 slices glacé pineapple (125g), chopped coarsely
- ⅓ cup (70g) each red and green glacé cherries, halved
- ⅓ cup (75g) coarsely chopped glacé ginger
- ½ cup (70g) slivered almonds, extra

ginger syrup
- ¾ cup (180ml) water
- ¾ cup (165g) caster (superfine) sugar
- 2 teaspoons finely grated fresh ginger

1 Preheat oven to 160°C/325°F. Grease a 12-hole (⅓-cup/80ml) muffin pan; line bases with baking paper. Sprinkle nuts into pan holes.

2 Beat butter, rind and sugar in a small bowl with an electric mixer until light and fluffy. Beat in eggs one at a time, until mixture is just combined.

3 Transfer mixture to a medium bowl; stir in sifted flours, milk, fruit and extra nuts. Spread mixture into pan holes. Bake about 25 minutes.

4 Meanwhile, make ginger syrup.

5 Remove cakes from oven; pour hot syrup over hot cakes in pan. Cool cakes in pan.

ginger syrup Stir ingredients in a small saucepan over medium heat, without boiling, until sugar dissolves; bring to the boil. Reduce heat; simmer, uncovered, without stirring, about 5 minutes or until syrup thickens slightly.

makes 12
prep + cook time
55 minutes (+ cooling)

Tip You can buy the fruit mince for this recipe or make your own (see cranberry & apple fruit mince, page 41).

mini fruit mince cakes

You need 1.5cm (¾-inch), 2cm (¾-inch) and 3cm (1¼-inch) star cutters.

- 1⅓ cups (200g) self-raising flour
- ⅓ cup (75g) firmly packed brown sugar
- 1½ cups (440g) fruit mince
- ½ cup (125ml) olive oil
- ⅓ cup (80ml) milk
- 1 egg
- ¼ cup (35g) cornflour (cornstarch), for dusting
- 250g (8 ounces) white ready-made icing
- cachous

1 Preheat oven to 200°C/400°F. Line 40 holes of four 12-hole (1-tablespoon/20ml) mini muffin pans with paper cases.
2 Sift flour and sugar into a large bowl.
3 Whisk fruit mince, oil, milk and egg in a medium bowl until combined; stir into flour mixture until barely combined.
4 Drop level tablespoons of mixture into pan holes; bake about 15 minutes. Cool cakes in pans.

5 On a surface dusted with cornflour, knead icing until smooth. Roll out into a 3mm (⅛-inch) thickness; cut out stars. Brush a tiny amount of water onto backs of stars; position on cakes. Press cachous into centres of stars before icing dries.

makes 40
prep + cook time
40 minutes (+ cooling)

greeting cards

If it's the thought that counts, then making your own greeting cards is a charming way to show someone that you've been thinking of them. This is no less true than at Christmas when we often reach out to friends and family who we haven't seen all year. So, rather than sending store-bought greeting cards, why not try your hand at making your own.

Handmade cards don't have to be time-consuming – you can decorate pre-made cards with an assortment of colourful buttons and ribbons. Before you start, choose a colour theme for your decorations (see gift wrapping, page 16) that matches the cards you've purchased. If you can't find pre-made cards to suit your style or colour, simply cut and fold lightweight cardboard.

Decorate the cards with simple patterns of buttons or trim the edges of each card with ribbon – the colours will be enough to make your greeting cards look festive. Next, you can try combining the buttons and ribbon to make Christmas motifs such as a tree or a star. Attach your decorations with clear-drying craft glue.

If you wish to mail your homemade cards to friends and family, remember to make them in sizes that will fit standard-sized envelopes. Some pre-made cards come with envelopes but you will need to buy envelopes for any cards that you cut from cardboard.

tip It is much easier to address the envelope before putting the card inside.

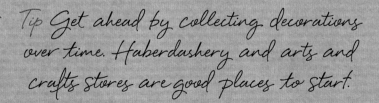

Tip Get ahead by collecting decorations over time. Haberdashery and arts and crafts stores are good places to start.

buttery almond & cranberry loaves

- 250g (8 ounces) butter, softened
- 1⅔ cups (370g) caster (superfine) sugar
- ½ teaspoon almond extract
- 6 eggs
- 300g (9½ ounces) sour cream
- 1¼ cups (185g) plain (all-purpose) flour
- 1¼ cups (185g) self-raising flour
- 1 cup (120g) ground almonds
- ¼ cup (60ml) orange juice
- 1½ cups (225g) dried sweetened cranberries
- icing (confectioners') sugar, for dusting

1 Preheat oven to 170°C/340°F. Grease two 8-hole (¾-cup/180ml) mini loaf pans; line base and long sides with baking paper, extending paper 2cm (¾-inch) above sides.

2 Beat butter, sugar and extract in a large bowl with an electric mixer until light and fluffy. Add eggs, one at a time, beating until just combined. Add cream, beat until just combined (don't overbeat the mixture).

3 Stir in sifted flours and ground almonds, then juice and cranberries. Divide mixture between pans; smooth tops; tap pans on bench to release air bubbles. Bake about 30 minutes. Stand cakes in pans 5 minutes before turning, top-side up, onto a wire rack to cool.

4 Serve cakes dusted with sifted icing sugar.

makes 16
prep + cook time
45 minutes

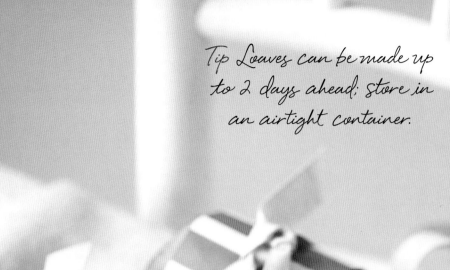

Tip Loaves can be made up to 2 days ahead; store in an airtight container.

Tips Panforte can be wrapped in layers of plastic wrap and stored in a dark dry place for up to 2 months. You will need 6 slices of glacé orange for this recipe.

jaffa panforte

- ⅔ cup (100g) plain (all-purpose) flour
- 1 cup (190g) coarsely chopped dried figs
- 1 cup (140g) coarsely chopped seeded dried dates
- 2 slices glacé orange (45g), chopped finely
- 1 cup (160g) blanched almonds, roasted
- 1 cup (140g) roasted hazelnuts
- 1 cup (140g) roasted macadamias
- ⅓ cup (115g) honey
- ⅔ cup (150g) firmly packed brown sugar
- 2 tablespoons Grand Marnier
- 100g (3 ounces) dark (semi-sweet) chocolate, melted
- 4 slices glacé orange (90g), extra

1 Preheat oven to 150°C/300°F. Grease four deep 10cm (4-inch) round cake pans; line bases with baking paper.
2 Sift flour into a large bowl; stir in fruit and nuts.
3 Stir honey, sugar and liqueur in a small saucepan over medium heat, without boiling, until sugar dissolves. Simmer, uncovered, without stirring, 5 minutes. Pour hot syrup, then chocolate into mixture; mix well.

4 Press mixture firmly into pans; top each with a slice of extra orange.
5 Bake panforte about 25 minutes; cool in pans. Remove panforte from pans; wrap in foil. Stand overnight.

makes 4
prep + cook time
1 hour (+ cooling)

microwave
Christmas puddings

- **125g (4 ounces) butter**
- **¾ cup (150g) firmly packed dark brown sugar**
- **2 eggs**
- **2 teaspoons golden syrup**
- **1¼ cups (250g) dried mixed fruit**
- **½ cup (110g) canned pie apples**
- **¾ cup (110g) plain (all-purpose) flour**
- **1 teaspoon mixed spice**
- **1 cup (70g) stale breadcrumbs**
- **¼ cup (60ml) sweet sherry**

brandy cream sauce
- **300ml thickened cream**
- **¼ cup (60ml) brandy**
- **2 eggs**
- **½ cup (110g) caster (superfine) sugar**

1 Make brandy cream sauce.

2 Grease six 1-cup (250ml) microwave-safe bowls.

3 Beat butter and sugar in a small bowl with an electric mixer until light and fluffy. Add eggs, one at a time, beating well between additions; beat in golden syrup.

4 Stir in fruit, pie apples, sifted flour and spice, breadcrumbs and sherry. Divide mixture between prepared bowls. Cook, uncovered, on LOW (30%) about 30 minutes or until cooked when a wooden skewer comes out clean. Stand 5 minutes before turning out onto a serving plate. Serve immediately with brandy cream sauce.

brandy cream sauce Beat cream and brandy in a medium bowl with an electric mixer until soft peaks form. Beat egg and sugar in a small bowl with an electric mixer until thick and creamy. Fold egg mixture into cream mixture.

serves 6
prep + cook time
50 minutes

tip Puddings can be made a week ahead; store, covered, in the fridge, or freeze for up to 2 months. Brandy cream sauce can be made a day ahead; store, covered, in the fridge.

tip The easiest way to line the base of the pan holes is to cut the bottom out of cupcake paper cases; use the correct sized case for the muffin pan.

gluten- & dairy-free spicy fruit cakes

- ⅓ cup (45g) slivered almonds
- ½ cup (105g) finely chopped mixed glacé cherries
- 2 tablespoons finely chopped glacé ginger
- ¼ cup (75g) finely chopped glacé pear
- 100g (3 ounces) dairy-free spread
- 1 cup (135g) gluten-free self-raising flour
- 1 teaspoon ground ginger
- ½ teaspoon ground cloves
- ½ cup (110g) firmly packed brown sugar
- ¼ cup (60ml) rice milk
- 1 egg
- 1 egg white

1 Preheat oven to 180°C/350°F. Grease a 12-hole (⅓-cup/80ml) standard muffin pan; line bases of pan holes with rounds of baking paper.

2 Combine nuts and glacé fruit in a small bowl; sprinkle mixture evenly into pan holes.

3 Beat spread in a small bowl with an electric mixer about 1 second, just to soften slightly (don't overbeat or it will break down). Sift flour, spices and 2 tablespoons of the sugar together. Beat flour mixture and milk into spread until just combined.

4 Beat egg and egg white in a small bowl with an electric mixer for 5 minutes or until thick and creamy. Add remaining sugar, beat until dissolved. Gradually beat egg mixture into flour mixture.

5 Divide mixture between pan holes. Bake cakes about 15 minutes. Stand cakes in pan 5 minutes before turning, bottom-side up, onto wire rack to cool.

makes 12
prep + cook time
35 minutes

ALMONDS flat, pointy-tipped nuts with a pitted brown shell enclosing a creamy white kernel covered by brown skin.

blanched brown skins removed.

flaked paper-thin slices.

ground also known as almond meal; nuts are powdered to a coarse flour texture, for use in baking or as a thickening agent.

slivered small pieces cut lengthways.

BICARBONATE OF SODA also known as baking soda; a mild alkali used as a leavening (raising) agent in baking.

BRANDY spirit distilled from wine.

BREADCRUMBS, STALE one- or two-day-old bread made into crumbs by blending or processing.

BUTTER we use salted butter; 125g is equal to one stick (4 ounces) of butter.

CACHOUS also called dragées in some countries; minuscule metallic-looking but edible confectionery balls used in cake decorating; available in silver, gold or various colours.

CARDAMOM a spice native to India and used extensively in its cuisine; can be purchased in pod, seed or ground form. Has a distinctive aromatic, sweetly rich flavour.

CHILLI generally, the smaller the chilli, the hotter it is. Use rubber gloves when seeding and chopping fresh chillies as they can burn your skin. Removing seeds and membranes lessens the heat.

cayenne pepper a long, thin-fleshed, extremely hot red chilli native to South America usually sold dried and ground.

long a generic term used for any moderately hot, long (6cm-8cm), thin chilli.

CHOCOLATE

Choc Bits also known as chocolate chips and chocolate morsels; available in milk, white and dark chocolate. Made of cocoa liquor, cocoa butter, sugar and an emulsifier, these hold their shape in baking and are ideal for decorating.

dark also known as semi-sweet or luxury chocolate; made of a high percentage of cocoa liquor and cocoa butter, and a little added sugar.

white contains no cocoa solids but derives its sweet flavour from cocoa butter. Very sensitive to heat, so watch carefully if melting.

CINNAMON STICK dried inner bark of the shoots of the cinnamon tree.

CLOVES dried flower buds of a tropical tree; can be used whole or in ground form. Have a strong scent and taste so should be used minimally.

COCONUT

desiccated concentrated, dried, unsweetened and finely shredded coconut.

shredded unsweetened thin strips of dried coconut.

CORIANDER also known as pak chee, cilantro or chinese parsley; bright-green leafy herb with a pungent flavour.

Also available ground or as seeds; these should not be substituted for fresh coriander as the tastes are completely different.

CORNFLOUR also known as cornstarch; used as a thickening agent in cooking. Available as 100% maize (corn) and as wheaten cornflour (wheaten has added gluten).

CRANBERRIES, DRIED have the same slightly sour, succulent flavour as fresh cranberries. Available in supermarkets.

CREAM we use fresh cream, also known as pure cream and pouring cream, unless otherwise stated; it has no additives unlike commercially thickened cream.

sour a thick commercially-cultured soured cream.

thickened a whipping cream containing a thickener.

CUMIN also known as zeera or comino; resembling caraway in size, cumin is the dried seed of a plant related to the parsley family. Its spicy, nutty, almost curry-like flavour is essential to the traditional foods of Mexico, India, North Africa and the Middle East. Available dried as seeds or ground.

CUMQUATS orange-coloured citrus fruit about the size of walnuts. Usually preserved or used for making jam, the skin is always retained.

CURRANTS, DRIED tiny, almost black raisins named after a grape variety that originated in Corinth, Greece.

glossary

DATES fruit of the date palm tree, eaten fresh or dried. About 4cm to 6cm in length, oval and plump, thin-skinned, with a honey-sweet flavour and sticky texture.

DUKKAH an Egyptian spice mixture made of roasted nuts, seeds and aromatic spices.

EDIBLE RICE PAPER made from the rice paper plant, not from rice; used in making confectionery. Not the same rice paper as used in Asian rice paper rolls. Available from selected kitchenware stores and some delicatessens.

FENNEL also known as finocchio or anise; a white to very pale green-white vegetable. Also the name given to dried seeds having a licorice flavour.

FIGS best eaten in peak season, at the height of summer. Figs are also glacéd (candied), dried or canned in sugar syrup; these are usually sold at health-food stores, Middle Eastern food shops or specialty cheese counters.

FLOUR

gluten-free self-raising uses starches containing no gluten (maize, tapioca, potato, rice) as well as raising agents.

plain all-purpose flour, made from wheat.

rice very fine flour, made from ground white rice.

self-raising also called self-rising, plain flour sifted with baking powder in the proportion of 1 cup flour to 2 teaspoons baking powder.

FRUIT MINCE a mixture of dried fruits such as raisins, sultanas and candied peel, nuts, spices, apple, brandy or rum. Used as a filling for cakes, puddings and fruit mince pies.

GELATINE a thickening agent made from either collagen, a protein found in animal connective tissue and bones, or certain algae (agar-agar). We use dried (powdered) gelatine; it's also available in sheet form known as leaf gelatine. 3 teaspoons of dried gelatine (8g or one sachet) is about the same as 4 gelatine leaves. The two types are interchangable but leaf gelatine gives a much clearer mixture than dried gelatine.

GINGER also known as green or root ginger; the thick root of a tropical plant.

glacé fresh ginger root preserved in sugar syrup. Crystallised ginger can be substituted if rinsed with warm water and dried before using.

ground also known as powdered ginger; cannot be substituted for fresh ginger.

GLACÉ FRUIT fruit such as cherries, peaches, pineapple and orange cooked in heavy sugar syrup then dried.

GLUCOSE SYRUP also known as liquid glucose, made from wheat or corn starch.

GOLDEN SYRUP a by-product of refined sugarcane; pure maple syrup or honey can be substituted.

GRAND MARNIER orange-flavoured liqueur based on cognac, a type of brandy.

HAZELNUTS also known as filberts; plump, grape-size, rich, sweet nuts having a brown inedible skin that is removed by rubbing heated nuts together vigorously in a tea towel.

IRISH WHISKEY a smooth, light, dry whiskey made from distilled fermented barley and other grains.

KAFFIR LIME LEAVES also known as bai magrood. Aromatic leaves of a citrus tree; two glossy dark green leaves joined end to end, forming a rounded hourglass shape. A strip of fresh lime peel may be substituted for each kaffir lime leaf.

KITCHEN STRING made of a natural product such as cotton or hemp so that it neither affects the flavour of the food it's tied around nor melts when heated.

MACADAMIAS rich and buttery nut native to Australia; store in refrigerator because of their high oil content.

MAPLE SYRUP a thin syrup distilled from the sap of the maple tree. Maple-flavoured syrup or pancake syrup is not an adequate substitute for the real thing.

MARSHMALLOWS made from sugar, glucose, gelatine and cornflour.

MIXED DRIED FRUIT a mix of sultanas, raisins, currants, mixed peel and cherries.

MIXED PEEL candied citrus peel.

MIXED SPICE a blend of ground spices usually consisting of cinnamon, allspice and nutmeg.

NIGELLA SEEDS also known as kalonji or black onion seeds; angular seeds, black on the outside and creamy within, having a sharp nutty flavour.

NUTMEG the dried nut of an evergreen tree native to Indonesia; it is available in ground form or you can grate your own with a fine grater.

PECANS golden-brown, buttery and rich nut native to the United States.

PISTACHIOS pale green, delicately flavoured nut inside hard off-white shells. To peel, soak shelled nuts in boiling water for about 5 minutes; drain, then pat dry with absorbent paper. Rub skins with cloth to peel.

PRUNES commercially or sun-dried plums.

RAISINS dried sweet grapes.

READY-MADE ICING also known as soft icing, ready-to-roll and prepared fondant.

RICE BUBBLES puffed rice product made with malt extract which contains gluten.

RUM we use a dark underproof rum (not overproof) for a more subtle flavour in cooking.

SHERRY fortified wine consumed as an aperitif or used in cooking; sold as fino (light, dry), amontillado (medium sweet, dark) and oloroso (full-bodied, very dark).

SOY SAUCE made from fermented soya beans. Several variations are available in most supermarkets and Asian food stores.

STERILISING JARS it's important to sterilise storage jars or bottles to prevent contamination and lengthen the shelf life of homemade jams, preserves and sauces. Jars that aren't sterilised properly can cause deterioration during storage. Make sure your hands, the preparation area, tea towels and cloths are clean too. The aim is to finish sterilising the jars and lids at the same time the preserve is ready to be bottled; the hot preserve should be bottled into hot, dry clean jars. Leave preserves at room temperature to cool before storing.

SUGAR

brown very soft, finely granulated sugar retaining molasses for its characteristic colour and flavour.

caster also known as superfine or finely granulated table sugar.

icing also known as confectioners' sugar or powdered sugar; granulated sugar crushed together with a small amount of cornflour.

pure icing no added cornflour.

raw natural brown granulated sugar.

white a coarse, granulated table sugar, also known as crystal sugar.

SULTANAS dried grapes, also known as golden raisins.

SWEETENED CONDENSED MILK a canned milk product from which 60% of the water has been removed; the remaining milk is then sweetened with sugar.

TREACLE thick, dark syrup not unlike molasses; a by-product of sugar refining. Golden syrup can be substituted but the flavour will be different.

TURKISH DELIGHT popular Middle Eastern sweet. Its Turkish name is rahat lokum – meaning 'rest for the throat'. A mixture of syrup and cornflour is boiled with either honey or fruit juice. Most often flavoured with rosewater or peppermint. Available from supermarkets.

VANILLA

bean dried long, thin pod from a tropical golden orchid grown in Central and South America and Tahiti; the tiny black seeds inside the bean are used to impart a luscious vanilla flavour in baking and desserts.

extract made by pulping chopped vanilla beans with a mixture of alcohol and water. This gives a very strong solution, so only a couple of drops are needed to flavour most dishes.

VINEGAR, APPLE CIDER made from cider or apple must.

WALNUTS the shell of the ripe nut is creamy brown with a striated surface; the kernel is ridged and oval and formed in two distinct halves.

conversion chart

measures

One Australian metric measuring cup holds approximately 250ml, one Australian metric tablespoon holds 20ml, one Australian metric teaspoon holds 5ml. The difference between one country's measuring cups and another's is within a 2- or 3-teaspoon variance, and will not affect your cooking results. North America, New Zealand and the United Kingdom use a 15ml tablespoon. All cup and spoon measurements are level. The most accurate way of measuring dry ingredients is to weigh them. When measuring liquids, use a clear glass or plastic jug with metric markings. We use large eggs with an average weight of 60g.

dry measures

METRIC	IMPERIAL
15g	½oz
30g	1oz
60g	2oz
90g	3oz
125g	4oz (¼lb)
155g	5oz
185g	6oz
220g	7oz
250g	8oz (½lb)
280g	9oz
315g	10oz
345g	11oz
375g	12oz (¾lb)
410g	13oz
440g	14oz
470g	15oz
500g	16oz (1lb)
750g	24oz (1½lb)
1kg	32oz (2lb)

liquid measures

METRIC	IMPERIAL
30ml	1 fluid oz
60ml	2 fluid oz
100ml	3 fluid oz
125ml	4 fluid oz
150ml	5 fluid oz
190ml	6 fluid oz
250ml	8 fluid oz
300ml	10 fluid oz
500ml	16 fluid oz
600ml	20 fluid oz
1000ml (1 litre)	1¾ pints

length measures

METRIC	IMPERIAL
3mm	⅛in
6mm	¼in
1cm	½in
2cm	¾in
2.5cm	1in
5cm	2in
6cm	2½in
8cm	3in
10cm	4in
13cm	5in
15cm	6in
18cm	7in
20cm	8in
23cm	9in
25cm	10in
28cm	11in
30cm	12in (1ft)

oven temperatures

These oven temperatures are only a guide for conventional ovens. For fan-forced ovens, check the manufacturer's manual.

	°C (CELSIUS)	°F (FAHRENHEIT)
Very slow	120	250
Slow	150	275-300
Moderately slow	160	325
Moderate	180	350-375
Moderately hot	200	400
Hot	220	425-450
Very hot	240	475

The imperial measurements used in these recipes are approximate only. Measurements for cake pans are approximate only. Using same-shaped cake pans of a similar size should not affect the outcome of your baking. We measure the inside top of the cake pan to determine sizes.

index

fresh new look
Mini cookbooks

THE AUSTRALIAN
Women's Weekly
Best-ever
BROWNIES

It's never the wrong time for brownies

THE AUSTRALIAN
Women's Week
Diet
SNACK

Healthy snacks to help you...

THE AUSTRALIAN
Women's Wee
VEGIES

...cious meat-free main meals

On sale at selected newsagents and supermarkets
or order online now at awwcookbooks.com.au